OIL

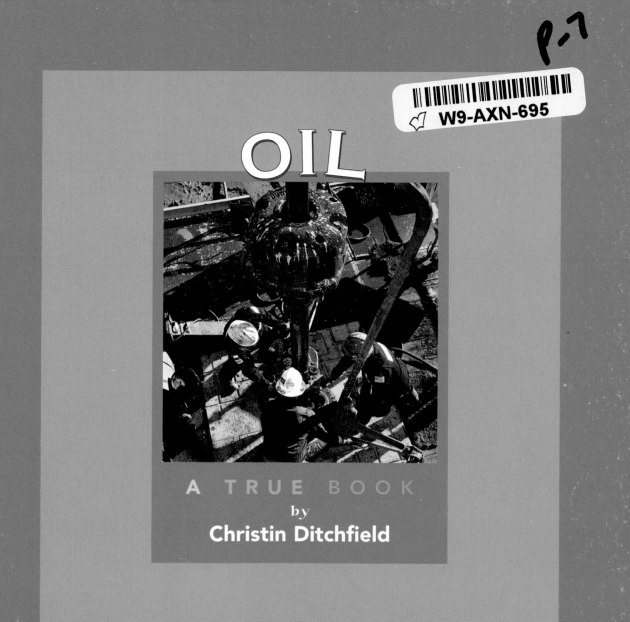

A TRUE BOOK

by

Christin Ditchfield

Children's Press®
A Division of Scholastic Inc.

New York Toronto London Auckland Sydney
Mexico City New Delhi Hong Kong
Danbury, Connecticut

Pipelines transport oil all over the world.

Content Consultant
Jan Jenner, Ph.D.

Reading Consultant
Linda Cornwell
National Literacy Specialist

Library of Congress Cataloging-in-Publication Data

Ditchfield, Christin.
    Oil / by Christin Ditchfield
        p.   cm.—(A True book)
    Includes bibliographical references and index.
    ISBN 0-516-22343-7 (lib. bdg.)   0-516-29367-2 (pbk.)
    1. Petroleum—Juvenile literature. [1. Petroleum.] I. Title. II. Series.
TN870.3 .D57 2002
553.2'82—dc21

                                                    2001023105

© 2002 by Children's Press
A Division of Scholastic Inc.
All rights reserved. Published simultaneously in Canada.
Printed in China.

CHILDREN'S PRESS, AND A TRUE BOOK®, and associated logos are
trademarks and or registered trademarks of Grolier Publishing Co., Inc.
SCHOLASTIC and associated logos are trademarks and or registered
trademarks of Scholastic Inc.

5 6 7 8 9 10 R 11 10 09 08 07   62

Contents

This dark, thick liquid is called oil.

What Is Oil?

Oil is sometimes called black gold. This thick, gooey liquid is one of our most valuable natural resources. A natural resource is a substance found in nature that has many important uses. The gas we use to fuel cars and trucks comes from petroleum oil.

Oil is delivered to homes and is used to fuel cars and trucks.

We also use oil to create heat for our homes and factories.

Oil is known as a **fossil fuel**. It comes from the remains of **decayed** plants and animals, which once lived in the sea. When these tiny creatures died, they sank to

Oil began as plants and animals thousands of years ago.

the bottom of the ocean floor. Layers of mud and sand covered the creatures. Over many years, the mud turned to rock. The heat and weight of the rock turned the remains of the creatures inside into little drops of the liquid we call oil.

Where Is Oil Found?

For almost two thousand years, people have been digging for oil. Oil is buried in layers of rock, deep below the Earth's surface. These layers can be found beneath the ocean or under dry land. Some people may imagine that the oil flows underground like a river, but scientists tell us that there are no pools of oil. The layers of rock trap tiny droplets of oil in the same way that a sponge traps water. When the rocks

Oil workers discover oil trapped in some rocks.

are broken up, they release the oil inside. The oil comes gushing out because it has been under tremendous pressure from the rocks. It is similar to what happens when you stick a pin into a balloon full of air— the air rushes out with a big bang! In the same way, drilling for oil causes it to spurt out of the ground with great force.

Geologists study the Earth to see where they might find oil. They have discovered oil on every continent except Antarctica. More than half of the world's oil is located in the Middle East. The United States, Russia, and Asia also have large supplies of oil.

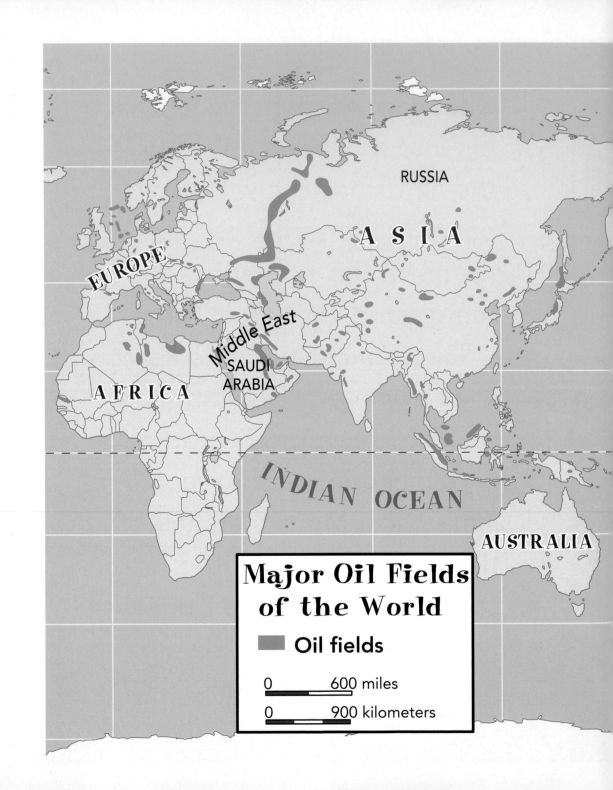

RUSSIA

A S I A

EUROPE

Middle East

SAUDI
ARABIA

AFRICA

INDIAN OCEAN

AUSTRALIA

Major Oil Fields of the World

Oil fields

0   600 miles

0   900 kilometers

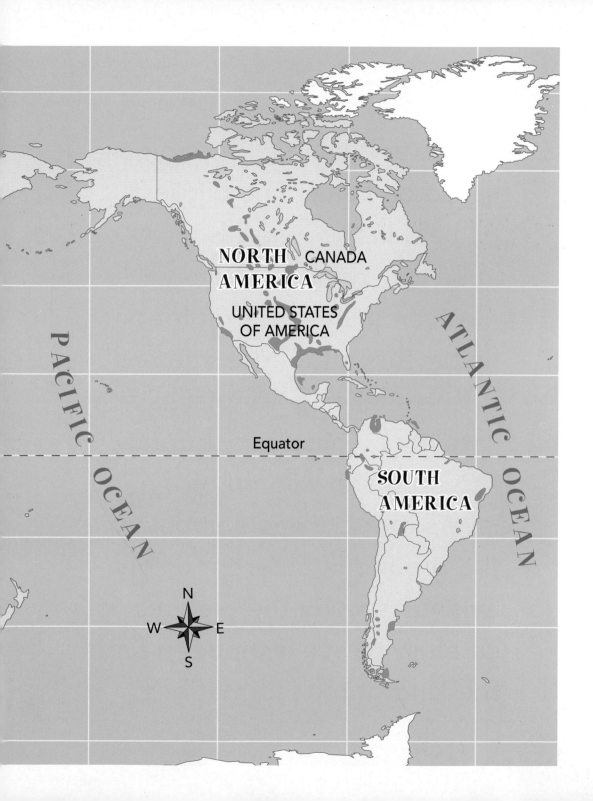

Places that have a lot of oil are called oil fields. The biggest oil field in the world is located in Saudi Arabia.

When scientists look for oil fields, they often use infrared pictures taken by airplanes and **satellites**. These special photographs show some of the layers of rocks and soil below the ground in different colors. Scientists study the pictures carefully to see if they can find the kind of rock formations

Scientists use seismographs, machines that take seismic readings, and computers to search for oil.

that may trap oil. There are other tests that scientists can use. A **seismic** survey measures shock waves coming from the ground. From the size and speed of these vibrations, scientists can tell if oil is there. Special machines detect gases in the air that help them to sniff out where oil is buried. These tests and machines really help scientists who are hunting for oil, but there is only one way to know for sure where oil is hidden. You have to dig!

How Oil Is Processed?

Geologists search for oil fields. When they find an oil field, an oil company takes over. The company's job is to bring the oil to the surface, where it can be put to use.

Engineers, people who design and build structures,

Oil company employees visit the site of future oil fields (above). An oil rig is built to support the huge drill that digs into the ground (right).

begin by building an oil rig over the spot where they plan to dig. An oil rig is a large tower that supports a big, metal drill. The rig also supports the engine that powers the drill. The oil drill is attached to a large pipe. The drill forces its way deep into the ground, cutting through layers of soil, sand, and rock. This creates a long, narrow tunnel called a shaft. As the shaft goes deeper,

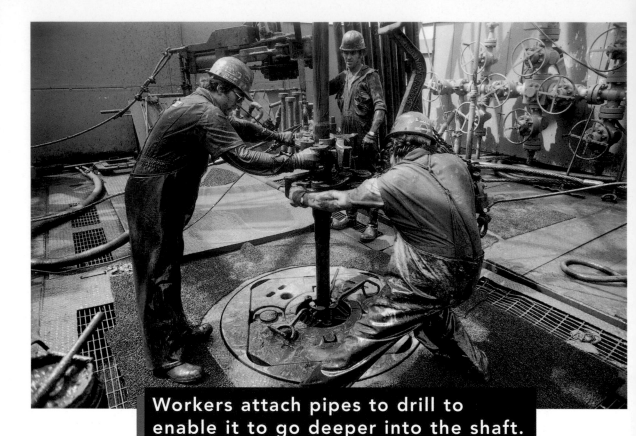

Workers attach pipes to drill to enable it to go deeper into the shaft.

workers attach longer pipes to the drill.

There are sharp metal teeth at the end of the drill, which are called drill bits.

These bits crush the rocks as the drill digs. If the drill bits hit rocks that hold oil, the oil will burst out of the crushed rocks and into the drill pipe.

The drill bits help the drill dig through rock.

This is an oil well pump, which helps get the oil out of the ground once it has been discovered.

Special pumps force the oil up the pipeline to the surface of the ground. From there, the oil is pumped into storage tanks or special pipelines that carry it away.

Oil that has just come from the ground is called crude oil. Crude oil looks black, dark green, or light yellow. This thick, slimy liquid cannot be

A manager and an oil technician discuss oil samples.

Oil is taken to a factory called a refinery (right). A worker monitors the equipment that processes the oil in the refinery's control room (above).

used for anything until it has been cleaned and prepared at a special factory called a refinery. An oil refinery has many pipes, tanks, and towers. Workers put the oil through several processes to clean it and prepare it for use.

Oil is actually made up of several different liquids, including gasoline, kerosene, hexane, and benzene. When oil is heated, these liquids can be separated from each other

An oil tanker unloads crude oil at a refinery.

and used for different things. Engineers heat oil in a fractioning tower that contains several compart-ments or sections. As the ingredients of oil separate, they are piped away to dif-ferent tanks. Special trucks and ships called oil tankers carry the oil to more facto-ries where it can be made into many things.

On the Job

It takes a lot of hard work to build an oil rig. The men and women who do this job are sometimes called roughnecks. They have special training to operate the heavy machines and keep them running properly. Once the drilling starts, it doesn't stop! The roughnecks take turns working day and night.

Because they work non-stop, the roughnecks on an offshore oil rig live right on the platform where they are drilling for oil. These platforms have offices, kitchens, rest rooms, and cabins where the workers sleep. Some rigs even have restaurants or a small movie theater where the workers can relax!

What Is Oil Used For?

Oil is one of our most important sources of fuel. It keeps us warm in the winter and allows us to travel wherever we want to go. All over the world, people burn oil to provide heat and energy to their homes and factories. Cars and trucks run on gasoline.

Cars, trucks, and planes depend on different forms of oil for fuel.

Trucks, trains, and buses use diesel fuel. Jet planes are powered by kerosene oil.

Once oil has been processed at the refinery, it can be used to make many different things. Scientists use oil to make plastic. All kinds of things are made from plastic combs, toothbrushes, videotapes, bowls, buckets, and toys. Oil is an ingredient in the material used to make rubber tires, shoes, nylon clothing, and carpets. Certain waxes made from oil products can be found in animal foods and chewing gum.

Oil is used to make many things, including rubber tires.

Certain kinds of chemicals are made from oil. These chemicals can be found in

Oil is used to make certain chemicals, which are found in detergent and paint.

medicines, **detergents**, paints, and fertilizers. **Lubricating oil** makes machines work smoothly. Whether we realize it or not, most of us use oil in some way every single day!

What Is Next?

Countries around the world use millions of barrels of oil each year. People depend on oil for fuel, energy, and many of the products they use every day. The way they use oil causes some problems, however. When oil is burned, it releases dangerous gases into the air. These gases

When oil is burned for fuel, dangerous gases are released, polluting the air.

can cause explosions. These gases pollute the air with chemicals that are harmful to people, plants, and animals. Oil is carried from one place to another through pipelines and in ships and trucks called oil tankers. A pipeline may burst, causing a

Transporting oil can be hazardous. Pipelines can break, and oil tankers can be damaged and leak oil into the seas and oceans.

dangerous explosion and polluting the environment. Large amounts of oil have been spilled into oceans through leaks in oil tankers. The leaking oil has killed fish, birds, and sea animals.

When oil has been burned for fuel, it cannot be recycled. It is gone forever. That is why scientists are always looking for better ways to process and use the precious oil that we have. Some are trying to find new sources of energy that may be safer and cleaner than oil. They are experimenting with cars that run on electricity or batteries rather than gasoline. Scientists have even found

People are experimenting with different sources of energy, such as electricity to run cars and solar power to warm homes.

that homes can be heated with solar energy, or energy from the sun.

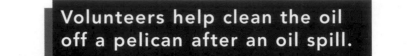
Volunteers help clean the oil off a pelican after an oil spill.

Volunteers interested in a clean environment often help to clean up oil spills and care for the animals and wildlife hurt by the spills. Others work to prevent accidents like these from happening in the first place. Together, we can take good care of the Earth and make the best use of our valuable natural resources.

Check It Out!

Scientists use detergent (soap) to clean up oil spills. Here is an experiment you can do to see how it works. You need:

A large bowl or bucket

Water

A long-handled spoon

Cooking oil

Liquid dishwashing detergent

1. Pour water into the bowl or bucket until it is at least half full.

2. Add two or three teaspoons of cooking oil. Stir the liquids with your spoon. Do they mix together?

3. Now add a squirt of dishwashing liquid. Stir the mixture again. What happens this time?

Detergent breaks up the oil so that it will **dissolve** into the water.

To Find Out More

Here are some additional resources to help you learn more about oil:

 **Books**

Bailey, Donna. **Energy from Oil and Gas.** Raintree Steck-Vaughn Publishers, 1995.

Brice, Raphaelle. **From Oil to Plastic.** Young Discovery Library, 1989.

Dineen, Jacqueline. **Oil, Gas, and Coal.** Raintree Steck-Vaughn Publishers, 1995.

Jackman, Wayne. **Gas.** Thomson Learning, 1993.

Rickard, Graham. **Oil.** Thomson Learning, 1993.

Smith, Roland. **Sea Otter Rescue, The Aftermath of an Oil Spill.** Penguin Putnam Books for Young Readers, 1999.

Spence, Margaret. **Fossil Fuels.** Gloucester Press/Aladdin Books, 1993.

Organizations and Online Sites

National Energy Information Center
1000 Independence Avenue S.W.
Washington, D.C. 20585
http://www.eia.doe.gov/kids/

This center offers interesting facts and other information about energy.

News and Directory for the Oil and Gas Industry
http://www.oil.com.

This online site provides the latest news, statistics, and information from oil companies at work.

Planetpals Earthzone
http://www.planetpals.com

This online site provides facts and fun activities about Earth.

United States Department of Energy
1000 Independence Avenue S.W.
Washington, D.C. 20585
http://www.energy.gov/kidz/kidzone.html

This government agency offers a special section for kids to learn more about energy.

United States Environmental Protection Agency
Explorers' Club for Kids
http://www.epa.gov/kids/

This online site combines facts with fun—games, contests, and ways you can help protect the environment.

Important Words

decay to rot away and fall apart

detergent a soap-like substance used to clean things

dissolve to break down and disappear

fossil fuels fuels formed when the remains of plants and animals are crushed under layers of sedimentary rock

geologist a scientist who studies rocks, minerals, and fossils to learn about the Earth

lubricating oil a thin type of oil used in machines to reduce friction between moving parts

satellite a spacecraft that circles the Earth

seismic something that involves the Earth's vibrations

Index

(**Boldface** page numbers
indicate illustrations.)

Meet the Author

Christin Ditchfield is the author of a number of books for Children's Press, including five True Books on natural resources. A former elementary school teacher, she is now a freelance writer and conference speaker, and host of the nationally syndicated radio program, *Take It To Heart!* Ms. Ditchfield makes her home in Sarasota, Florida.